RABBITS
AS A NEW PET
BARRY MARTIN

CONTENTS

Photos by Bruce Crook, Marvin Cummings, Michael Gilroy, Ray Hanson, H. Jesse, Burkhard Kahl, H. Reinhard, Mervin F. Roberts, D.G. Robinson, Vince Serbin, Louise Van der Meid.

9 8 7 6 5 4 3 2 1   **1996 Edition**   9 5   7 8 9

Distributed in the UNITED STATES to the Pet Trade by T.F.H. Publications, Inc., One T.F.H. Plaza, Neptune City, NJ 07753; distributed in the UNITED STATES to the Bookstore and Library Trade by National Book Network, Inc. 4720 Boston Way, Lanham MD 20706; in CANADA to the Pet Trade by H & L Pet Supplies Inc., 27 Kingston Crescent, Kitchener, Ontario N2B 2T6; Rolf C. Hagen Ltd., 3225 Sartelon Street, Montreal 382 Quebec; in CANADA to the Book Trade by Vanwell Publishing Ltd., 1 Northrup Crescent, St. Catharines, Ontario L2M 6P5 ; in ENGLAND by T.F.H. Publications, PO Box 15, Waterlooville PO7 6BQ; in AUSTRALIA AND THE SOUTH PACIFIC by T.F.H. (Australia), Pty. Ltd., Box 149, Brookvale 2100 N.S.W., Australia; in NEW ZEALAND by Brooklands Aquarium Ltd. 5 McGiven Drive, New Plymouth, RD1 New Zealand; in Japan by T.F.H. Publications, Japan—Jiro Tsuda, 10-12-3 Ohjidai, Sakura, Chiba 285, Japan; in SOUTH AFRICA by Lopis (Pty) Ltd., P.O. Box 39127, Booysens, 2016, Johannesburg, South Africa. Published by T.F.H. Publications, Inc.

MANUFACTURED IN THE UNITED STATES OF AMERICA
BY T.F.H. PUBLICATIONS, INC.

Natural History

For many years the rabbit was believed to be a member of the larger order of animals known as Rodentia — the rodents. It is now realized that this is not so. Any resemblance to rodents is the result of convergent evolution. This is when unrelated animals develop similar features as a result of living in similar environments and following similar lifestyles.

A pair of European rabbits in the wild.

Rabbits probably have more in common with hoofed animals than with rodents. Certainly the study of their blood cells suggests this. However, the exact relationship of rabbits and hares to other animals is still not known. Rabbits are now placed in their own order, Lagomorpha.

Fossil evidence of lagomorphs can be traced back to the Eocene period (about 50 million years ago). Most of today's species evolved during the late Pliocene period (about 2-3 million years ago). Many of today's mammals were speciating then.

The order Lagomorpha is divided into two families. One contains the rabbits and hares (Leporidae), and the other the pikas (Ochotonidae). The latter animals have short ears and legs. As a group, they are probably past their evolutionary zenith and are declining in numbers. Conversely, rabbits and hares are probably now at their peak. The family Leporidae comprises some 11 genera and 38 species. Ten of the genera and 17 of the species are rabbits; all hares are listed in a single genus, *Lepus*. The distinction between hares and

The rabbit has been kept by man for centuries, for its meat and fur as well as for its companionship.

rabbits is one of anatomy. Hares have longer limbs and ears. Also, they have 48 chromosomes (European hare), compared to the rabbit's (Old World rabbit) 44.

TEETH

The half jaw dental formula of the lagomorphs is:

$$\frac{2 - 0 - 3 - 3}{1 - 0 - 2 - 3} = \text{28 teeth in a full jaw}$$

This varies depending on if the animal has two less molars in the upper jaw, thus giving only 26 teeth. The large pair of teeth you see in the upper front jaw are called incisors. Behind these are a smaller pair. There are no canine teeth. The molars are used in a lateral chewing manner, rather like you see in a cow. The incisors continually grow. They are kept in check by their rubbing action against each other. It sometimes happens that they are not aligned correctly. In the wild state, such animals eventually starve to death, as the teeth grow to such a length that the animal cannot feed.

DISTRIBUTION

Lagomorphs are found throughout Eurasia, the Americas and the Far East.

They were absent from Australia, New Zealand, certain South American countries and many islands until introduced by man. Rabbits are especially adaptable to varying climatic conditions. As such, they quickly reach plague populations if there are no natural enemies or natural barriers to control their spread.

DOMESTIC RABBITS

This book is concerned only with the rabbit species *Oryctolagus cuniculus,* the Old World rabbit. It is from this species that all present-day rabbit breeds have been

European wild rabbit. Women of the Roman empire prized rabbit meat for its supposed cosmetic qualities.

produced. The Old World rabbit was spread throughout much of Europe at one time. Its habitat shrank with the advance of the last Ice Age until it was found only in Spain. In the Middle Ages it began to spread back to its former ranges.

COLONY LIFE

Wild rabbits live in colonies, varying from only a few to hundreds of residents. Unlike hares, which build their dens on the ground surface, rabbits dig many tunnels to form a warren. Rabbits prefer dry grassland to hard or damp earth. The warren's numerous tunnels lead to communal chambers and various dead-ends. Rabbits have a complicated social structure based on hierarchy. Does of senior rank build their nests in the main warren; those of lower rank build a short distance away.

Hearing is the prime rabbit sense. Sight is also good, and probably superior to that of a hare. The voice is a high pitched warning signal. Since six wild rabbits consume as much food as a single sheep, they are a serious problem to farmers.

Rabbits follow well-known trails if they have a need to escape a predator. They can attain speeds of approximately 35kph (21mph) and are adept at making rapid turns in direction. After the chase, rabbits usually attempt to get back to their burrows via the quickest route. The colony feeds mainly in the early morning hours and at dusk.

A lovely English Spot rabbit. This variety is also known as the English Butterfly rabbit.

Rabbits and Man

The domestication of rabbits must be attributed to the monks of French monasteries. They devoted considerable time to the selective breeding of rabbits to improve meat production potential. With selective inbreeding being practiced, color mutations eventually appeared. These were retained and improved upon. By the 16th century, a number of breeds had been established. It is also interesting to consider earlier records of man's contact with the wild rabbit.

The Phoenicians, famed for their sailing and trading, landed in Spain about 1100 BC. They saw the large numbers of rabbits, but were unfamiliar with the animals. The Phoenicians assumed them to be species of the hyrax (order Hyracoidea). These are small, rodent-like animals found in Africa. They gave the rabbits the name "shephan." This is Semitic for "one who hides," or hyrax as they knew it. They then called this new land "i-shephan-im," meaning land of the hyrax. From this came the later Latin translation of Hispania, to become Espana. To non-Spaniards, this is Spain.

The Romans were instrumental in the spread of the rabbit. It was a convenient food for their armies as they pushed northward through Europe. They also introduced it to many islands with such success that the local populations were forced to leave. Sometimes the emperor's help was called for to assist in reducing the numbers.

It became fashionable in Italy to keep rabbits and hares in leporaria. This trend was continued down through the Middle Ages by nobility. By this time, rabbit hunting was a popular sport. Rabbit was also an expensive dish to eat. The monks were allowed to eat unborn or newly born rabbits, known as laurice, during fasting. This was because the laurice were not considered meat. They were a delicacy dating back to the Romans.

The rabbit was introduced in Britain by the Normans shortly after their conquest of England during the 11th century. There it quickly found favor for both its meat and pelt. Ironically, the wild rabbit did not appear in Germany until some 300 years after the domestic strains.

The rabbit readily established itself wherever it was taken. It was introduced in Australia in 1797. It was not until 1859, when a re-introduction of British rabbits took place, that Australia's epic plague of rabbits was put in motion. Likewise, in spite of the catastrophic experience of Australia, rabbits were introduced in the 20th century to Chile. Here they also became a major pest. Their presence even endangered the Patagonian cavy (guinea pig), a native animal of that country.

A group of rabbits. Domestication and color breeding of rabbits was begun by the French. From there, the hobby spread to England, Scandinavia, and the rest of the world.

Rabbits were introduced to the Antarctic region and flourished. They upset the local balance of nature by the great amount of vegetation they consumed. During winter months they survived by adapting their feeding habits to include seaweed that had washed ashore.

MYXOMATOSIS

This infamous disease was named by Professor Sanereli. It prevails only in Old World rabbits, *Oryctolagus*. It is no longer common in domestic breeds, though they are at risk if suitable precautions are ignored. The history of the disease is of interest to rabbit owners.

In South America, a disease rarely fatal to wild rabbit species was transmitted to domestic rabbits housed at a Montevideo (Uruguay) hospital. All the rabbits died. Further outbreaks occurred in stock as far away as Brazil and California. In 1942, Aragoa concluded years of research. He stated that the disease was transmitted via mosquitoes and other flying insects. Concurrent with Aragoa's work, the Cambridge researcher, Dr. Charles Martin, conducted experiments. His studies occurred on the islands of Skokholm and Skomer, off the Welsh coast. Nearly all the Skokholm rabbits infected by Martin died. No others on that island died. On Skomer, only a short distance away, rabbits died in large numbers.

Attempts were made as early as 1927 in Australia to infect the rabbit population in arid zones. Alas, there was no success. Following Aragoa's work, further experiments were carried out in 1950. These were rendered in humid river areas where mosquitoes were plentiful; the rabbits died by the thousands. The fact that no success came in arid areas seemed to have supported Aragoa's work. The French entomologist, Dr. Armand Delille, was not convinced, though. He infected wild rabbits on his estate. They died in large numbers. Yet his domestic stock, exposed to mosquitoes as much as the wild population, did not die. This experiment took place in June 1952. By October, rabbits 60 kilometers away were found dead of the disease. It spread throughout France during the following years, including domestic breeds in its ranks. Delille announced his work in a paper to the French Agriculture Academy in 1953. He became the hero of farmers; the disease wiped out 45% of the wild rabbit population. Thirty-five percent of all domestic rabbits also died.

The irony of the story is that Delille was sued by the Conseil Superieure de la Chasse. This agency issued the hunting licenses which accounted for millions of dollars of government revenue. The number one prey for the hunters

An adult Dutch rabbit with juvenile spotted rabbits.

was rabbit. The revenue took a massive tumble and the Conseil won their case in the trial court. However, a higher court squashed the verdict. The ground was that it was not illegal, under French law, to introduce animal epidemics. A law passed in 1955 ensured this result. Subsequently, Delille received an award from the Agricultural Academy for his

work. However, he remained hated by sportsmen and rabbit breeders.

By the fall of 1953, the disease reached Britain. It quickly swept through the rabbit population. The Ministry of Agriculture experimented to determine the cause. Delille was convinced that the disease was spread by the rabbit flea, *Spilopsyllus cuniculi*, or similar arthropods. The Ministry confirmed that fleas, not mosquitoes, were the main carriers. This explained why the Skokholm test failed: the rabbits on Skokholm had no fleas, while those on Skomer did. Likewise, the rabbits of Australia's arid hinterland suffered far less with fleas than those in the more populated humid zones.

For a variety of reasons, vast sums of money were lost while myxomatosis was at its peak. France was a major rabbit meat consumer; pelts were sold in great numbers from many European countries. Britain's consumption of rabbit meat fell sharply and has never really recovered. Such has been the effect of the popular little rabbit the world over.

Wild rabbits are now largely immune to the disease. Therefore, wild populations are rapidly growing wherever the rabbit is seen. In future years, man will again be faced with the problem of how to impede the success of these adaptable creatures.

Accommodations

The type of housing selected for your rabbits is determined by a number of factors: 1) the number of rabbits kept; 2) whether they are housed indoors or out; 3) the available space; 4) the amount of money to be expended.

Almost any container makes a home of sorts for a rabbit. Old tea chests, orange boxes and crudely made hutches are all homes to pets. In any event, a rabbit given considerable free-running time is far better off than one permanently confined in superior quarters. A hutch can never be large enough to act as an exercising area, no matter how big.

A good home provides an eating area, sleeping quarters and is sheltered from inclement weather. The sleeping area is warm and dark, equating a natural situation. A rabbit can be kept in superb health simply by applying good hygiene rules and a correct diet. This does not

mean that the rabbit is ideally content. A rabbit needs as much free space to run and play in as possible.

THE HUTCH

Excellent hutches are available both for single pets and for breeders. Companies which manufacture these accommodations advertise in rabbit magazines. However, these hutches seem rather

Proper housing is a must if your pet is to live a long, healthy life.

expensive in comparison to those sold in pet shops. Other alternatives are to build your own hutch, or to have a carpenter do it to your specifications.

Single Outdoor Hutch: A substantial outdoor hutch is made from solid timber, either tongued and grooved, or 1.25cm (.5in) thick chipboard. This is then coated with a glossy, non-lead based paint for ease of cleaning. One of the coated woods can be used for the sides, back and roof, as these are easy to wipe clean. Because they are slippery, however, they are not good for the base. It is better if the panels are screwed to a

framework. This way the hutch can be dismantled if needed, or single panels can be removed and replaced.

Natural woods can be painted with a wood preservative or creosote. This prolongs the hutch life. It is essential that the floor is given extra coats of paint because rabbit urine is very strong. The wood will soon become rotted if left unprotected. Metal or plastic trays can be used, but these seem to be more trouble than they are worth.

The roof line should slope down from the front so rain is carried off. An overhang all around makes the hutch even

Example of a breeder block set-up. Note how the individual compartments are contained in one unit.

more attractive. A heavy-duty roofing felt gives extra protection; those in green are more attractive than normal black or red.

The hutch should be mounted on legs about 46cm (18in) high. This gives ample air space below the hutch so that routine cleaning can be done without your having to bend down. Two compartments should be incorporated in the hutch: one a feeding and rest area, the other for sleeping. A good ratio is one-third for sleeping and the rest for feeding. This, though, depends on how big the hutch is. These areas can be made by having a fixed partition built. A more favored approach is to insert a sliding panel in which a door has been cut.

A solid door should be attached to the sleeping area. This can be opened for cleaning and left closed to give the rabbit a cozy compartment. The rest of the hutch is usually covered with welded wire. The welded wire is placed on the inside of the frame to discourage gnawing. A stout gauge, 19G or even lower, is very strong. A

section of the wire is cut and put on a frame to form a door. The door can be hinged to open up, down or to the side.

It is better for the hutch to stand on a concrete base rather than bare earth. Paving slabs can also be used. These should extend well beyond the hutch area to facilitate cleaning. This way any wood shavings, rabbit droppings or food that falls can easily be swept away. The hutch should be situated near a fence or wall where it receives further protection from the weather. It should face away, at an angle, from the point that receives the most sunlight. A rabbit must always be able to escape the heat of direct sunlight.

Outdoor accommodations should be made of the finest materials. They must be completely draft-proof and free from dampness. Rabbits can cope with cold weather, but not with damp or drafty quarters. Their bedding should be thick and fresh at all times.

Indoor Hutch: The above comments are applicable to indoor hutches as well. There is no need to have the roof so well insulated or to have an overhang. Likewise, the sides do not need to be as thick as for outdoor housing. The floor should be similar.

Breeder Blocks: Breeder blocks need to be arranged in tiers if you plan to keep a substantial number of rabbits. Remember to leave adequate air space below the hutches. It is normal for banks of hutches to be complete units in themselves, that is, with fixed units. However, you should incorporate a few with sliding divisions. These can be opened up to provide a long unit for young stock or to give more room to pairs. In such a case, removable sleeping boxes can be incorporated. Always have at least one spare hutch in a unit so that the rabbits can be moved around by rotation. The spare hutch can be left empty for a minimum of ten days for thorough cleaning. Treat it with a suitable acaricide or insecticide. An isolation hutch,

Straw and hay are commonly used as bedding materials for rabbits.

as far from your stock as possible, is also a wise precaution.

Wire Cages: Commercial breeders have used all-wire cages for many years. These are now being used by domestic breeders. The advantage is that they are very hygienic and relatively inexpensive to construct. Of course, they are only suitable for indoor use. Another disadvantage is that they afford no privacy to the rabbits. They are also unattractive.

Size of Hutch: The size of the hutch depends to a great extent on the breed of rabbit. Dwarf breeds need less space than the Flemish giants. A typical size is 122cm (48in) by 46cm (18in) by 46cm (18in). An outdoor hutch is usually larger in dimension.

Morant Hutches: The morant hutch was designed to allow rabbits to graze on grass on a rotational basis. The normal shape of the hutch is triangular, but it can also be oblong. It is attached to a wire frame. The entire unit can be moved daily to a new feeding ground. In this way, the rabbit can be left outside during the day in complete safety from dogs, cats or foxes. If of a suitable size and strength, the hutch can be a permanent home for one or two rabbits. For extra safety, the base should be netted to prevent the rabbit from digging under the edge. The rabbit is able to graze on the grass that comes through the netting.

RABBIT ROOMS

You will no doubt use an outbuilding for your stock if you keep large numbers of rabbits outside. The addition of water and electric facilities enables chores to be done in comfort and at night. Such additions should be done by

Red Rex rabbit. Special food hoppers and water dishes and bottles made specifically for hutches are available at your local pet shop.

professionals. Be sure to get the approval of local authorities and inspectors.

Foods should be stored in airtight and waterproof containers. A table area for inspecting your stock is useful.

operate. Battery operated models are also available.

EXERCISE

All rabbits need as much exercise as possible. Outdoor exercise is better than indoor

Heat is not required for rabbits provided the accommodations are cozy. You, however, might appreciate having it. Ionizers are popular with bird keepers and are also suitable for rabbit owners. An ionizer discharges negative ions which adhere to dust and airborne protozoans. Thus, the risk of disease is minimized. Ionizers are not expensive to purchase or to

exercise. However, it is often impractical to let your pets run loose; they may escape or be difficult to catch. A good idea is to fence off a section of yard. This way the bunnies are contained and yet have ample room to play.

Leporaria: No doubt that rabbits are at their best in leporaria or enclosures where they can both live and play.

Such an enclosure can be surrounded by a wall or chainlink fence. The fencing should be sunk into the ground

and inwards to prevent the rabbits from burrowing out at the edge. Likewise, the fencing is better when supported by angular iron set in concrete. A slabbed path around the perimeter gives the whole area a neat look. A tree provides shade and adds to the overall effect. Shrubs can be added if they are encased at their base with fine gauge netting. This discourages the rabbits from nibbling at them. Rabbits kept in such a manner are hardier than any kept indoors. They can cope with just about any type of weather, including that of winter.

BEDDING

The base of the hutch can be covered with a variety of materials. Sawdust soaks up urine well, but it clings to the rabbits and their food. It can also create nose and eye problems. Wood shavings do not cling as much. However, more is needed to cover the floor. Paper soaks up urine well, but it sticks to the floor. Straw, meadow grass and hay are also all suitable.

Sable-point Dwarf Lop rabbit, an adult doe (left), with a Frosty-point Dwarf Lop juvenile female (right).

Stock Selection

Regardless of whether you want a rabbit as a pet or for breeding and exhibition, ensure that it is healthy. The next two important factors are its breed and its health quality.

HEALTH

An unhealthy rabbit is not difficult to spot. It is listless and exhibits other symptoms of poor health.

Conditions: Do not purchase a rabbit from a dealer with unclean cages. Dirty feeding pots, algae in drinking bottles and general untidiness increase the risk of problems.

General Look: Observe the rabbits for a few moments. They should have an alert look about them. Do not purchase a specimen that lies huddled in a corner and appears to be under the weather. A healthy rabbit should hop about effortlessly.

Head: The eyes of a rabbit should be round, clear and have a sparkle. Any sign of discharge could indicate a problem. The ears should be erect (except flop-eared breeds) and smell clean. Signs of abrasions or of brownish matter are undesirable. The teeth must be

Blue (left), Black (center), and Siamese (right) Smoke Pearl rabbits. In rabbit terminology, black is often called Marten.

aligned correctly; the upper teeth should overlap and just touch the lower teeth.

Body: The fur should be smooth and sleek. No signs of bald patches, fleas or lice should be present. Rub the fur against its lie to inspect the skin, especially around the neck, ears and above the tail. The anal region should be free of staining. The inside of the front legs should be dry with no sign of wet or matted fur. The feet should be clean and well formed.

CHOICE OF BREED

A novice is not recommended to take on varieties requiring special care of the coat or ears. Considerable time must be devoted to treatment. Large breeds may be more difficult for younger children to handle. However, they are often quite docile and make excellent pets. A purebred is not required if the rabbit is wanted simply as a pet. Almost any rabbit makes a fine companion. Fortunately, nearly all purebreds are modestly priced in comparison to other domestic pets, such as dogs, cats and birds.

Age: Rabbits are best purchased when they are about eight to ten weeks old. By this time they should be weaned. If handled often and gently, they become great tame pets. One can be trained to follow you about, come when called and let you pick it up without a struggle. In addition, breed

White Netherland Dwarf giving itself a bath. A healthy rabbit will take pride in its appearance and will be alert and aware of what's going on around it.

characteristics will usually become evident at this age. Breeding stock is best purchased as young adults (three months of age or older). At this time the nature of the markings is better judged.

Quality rabbits carry a leg band or ear tattoo. From this their history can be checked. It is not necessary to buy the most expensive stock. Your choice, though, must be of sound quality on which you can build

Broken Fawn Dwarf Lop buck (top left); Chinchilla Dwarf Lop doe (top right); Tortoiseshell English Lop doe (bottom left); and a Broken Madagascar French Lop doe (bottom right).

21

English Spot rabbit, black variety.

prime stock. Fortunately, even young show winning stock is reasonably priced.

Quality: You need to contact a breeder of the desired variety if you plan to breed and show stock. Such rabbits cost a bit more and may not be seen in pet stores. Visit a local rabbit show or write to the national governing body to find out about breeders in your area.

A pet shop may also have some information.

Netherland Dwarf rabbit.

Feeding

A quartet of Dutch rabbits having a meal. Proper nutrition is essential for all animals, and rabbits are no exception.

Rabbits are probably the easiest of all pets to feed. Much of the diet can be provided at very low cost by feeding foods already in the home or grown in the garden. All food items fall into one of three major constituent groups: carbohydrates, proteins and fats. Carbohydrates provide energy for muscular activity. Proteins build body tissue. Fats store reserves of energy, insulate the body from temperature changes and aid in the absorption of other requirements assisting in bodily functions. These other requirements are vitamins and minerals. These are needed in much smaller amounts than the major foods. Without them, though, an animal quickly

succumbs to illness. The final dietary item is water. Although many food sources contain water, a rabbit needs to have fresh water available at all times. More water is lost via perspiration, urine and fecal waste than is provided in food.

All of these nutritional requirements are found within cereals, green foods and vegetables. If foods are given in variety, vitamin supplements are not necessary. Indeed, excessive use of additives can do more harm than good.

Imbalances can be created that interfere with normal body metabolism.

CEREALS

These provide the bulk of carbohydrate content of the diet. Those most commonly given to rabbits are whole or crushed oats, bran, maize and barley. These are best served as a mix, with oats and bran being in the largest ratio. Other household cereals, such as corn flakes and shredded wheat, can be added to the mix. Bread, which has been hard baked or toasted, can be cut into pieces and added as well.

Mash: Dry cereal moistened with hot water or milk is termed a mash. This is appreciated as an alternative to a dry mix. It is often fed to pregnant and lactating does. A few drops of cod liver oil ensure that there is no shortage of vitamin C. This is particularly beneficial during the winter months when the amounts of sunlight are at their shortest. Mashes, however, sour quickly. Any uneaten mash should be removed once the rabbits lose interest in it.

Pellets: Commercially prepared pellets are available

from pet stores. They contain all of the nutritional needs of a rabbit in a scientific ratio. Water consumption rises if dry pellets are fed to your stock.

FEEDING DISHES

Both plastic and aluminum pots are available for rabbits. However, rabbits take great delight in tossing lightweight food dishes around. An earthenware container is therefore recommended. Your local pet shop will have a wide variety of both food and water dishes from which to choose.

GREEN FOOD

Green food provides both protein, vitamins and minerals. A vast range is available, both cultivated and wild growing. The outer leaves of cabbage and cauliflower, spinach, celery, peas and beans are excellent green foods.

Germinated seeds are

Tortoiseshell rabbit. A healthy, well-fed rabbit will be active and attentive.

particularly high in protein content. They are especially good for does rearing young. Simply soak some seeds in water for 24–36 hours. Wash them and place on a tray lined with blotting paper. Place the tray in a warm, dark area for another 24 hours. By this time small shoots should appear on the seeds. Wash the sprouts and serve them to your rabbits.

Wild Plants: Dandelion is the most popular plant given to rabbits. An excess of this or any other plant should be avoided.

Each has its own properties, some being laxatives, others astringents. One balances the other if a variety offered. Other common wild plants that are safe to feed to rabbits are clover, comfrey, thistles, plantain, shepherd's purse, yarrow, coltsfoot, chickweed, groundsel, bramble and dock. Many others are found in different countries. Keep in mind that rabbits do not eat only wild plants; they are partial to certain flowers as well.

Be aware that diarrhea is easily induced in the spring by the sudden rise in available plants. Feed plants carefully on a build-up process; likewise, reduce as autumn approaches. Lawn trimmings are enjoyed, but do not offer them to a rabbit if insecticides have been used. Additionally, do not collect wild plants from areas subject to car fumes and fouling by other animals. Remember to wash all green food before giving them to your pets.

Poisonous Plants: Few animals eat plants that are poisonous. However, precautions should be taken.

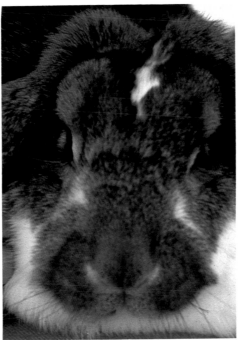

A good diet helps your pet maintain its wonderful eyesight and luxuriant coat.

Foxglove, larkspur, privet, poppy, hemlock and ivy must be avoided. Do not feed any plants which are grown from bulbs. These, too, are dangerous.

FRUITS AND VEGETABLES

Most fruits and vegetables are happily received by rabbits. These can be given, cut into cubes, as a mixed salad. Apples, grapes, pears, oranges and strawberries are enticing. Carrots, beet root, sugar beets, swedes and parsnip, together with root crops, can be offered.

HAY

Rabbits should be supplied with as much fresh hay as possible. Hay is good bedding as well as good food. The quality of hay varies; that sold in pet shops is usually excellent.

FEEDING TIME

Opinions differ among breeders as to whether rabbits should be fed once or twice a day. Once in the early evening, with tidbits provided during the day, seems to be adequate. The important thing is to establish a regular time of feeding.

WATER

Water can be supplied in earthenware pots or gravity fed bottles.

Bottles are superior; the water cannot be spilled or fouled with urine or droppings. Those with metal tips last longer. The bottles are attached to the hutch wires by metal or plastic clips. The spout goes through the wires so the rabbit can lick at it. During freezing weather, the tips often clog. Check the bottles regularly and maybe supply an extra water pot in the hutch. Clean and refill the bottles daily.

REFECTION (COPROPHAGY)

Rabbits, along with hares, shrews and other herbivores, may eat their own feces. Actually, those eaten are not the normal feces containing waste products of the digestive system. Rather, they are special pellets of partially digested food. What happens is that food passes

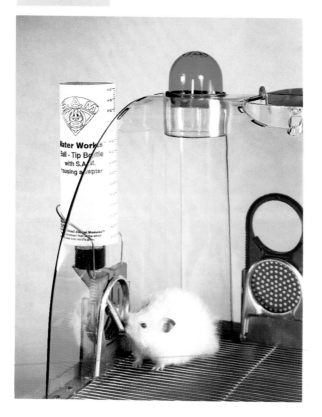

then passes along the colon and out through the rectum as fecal pellets. These are re-eaten and mix with the new food intake. They probably help start the breakdown of food, especially plant cellulose. This is because the pellets contain bacterial enzymes. Normal fecal droppings are then passed out.

into the stomach for digestion. Not all the food, though, is assimilated into the body. Some passes on through the system to the cecum. Here, bacteria act on it and important vitamins of the B complex are synthesized. It

TIDBITS

Avoid feeding very sweet items, such as candy, to your pets. Tidbits should be choice foods, like cheese, egg, raisins and the like.

Black English Lop chewing some hay. Note the extra-long ears on this fellow.

Breeding

Rearing rabbits carries its own excitement---self-bred exhibition winners are always more satisfying than those bred by other people. However, before breeding rabbits, some practical considerations must be made: Do you have time to devote to the increased number of animals? Do you have the available space? Can you afford the cost of breeding without cutting back on the quality and quantity of food? What are you going to do with all of the new youngsters?

If the above points do not pose a problem, the next

question is: How good is your stock? It costs as much to rear inferior specimens as it does to breed quality stock. Since rabbits are not so expensive anyway, financially it is more prudent to breed only from purebred animals of sound type. Such animals are easier to sell. Additionally, from a trio of purebreds, a stud of progressively better rabbits can be developed.

THE BUCK

The buck is the most important animal in any stud of rabbits. This is not because he can pass on more of his good qualities than can a female. Rather, it is because he gets a greater opportunity to do so. Thus, his standing points can be perpetuated rapidly in a given population. Therein lies the sting: if he carries an unknown fault (a recessive not shown visually), this is spread extensively within that population. A good stud can be assessed only by the number of quality progeny he produces consistently in ratio to the number of young he produces. This, of course, is affected by the quality of females to which he is mated. Simply using the

Young Dutch rabbit.

finest looking male is no guarantee that he can pass on his virtues. His track record must show that he can. This is a trap many beginners fall into. Therefore, only use a buck whose pedigree suggests that he is genetically as good as his appearance. If purchasing a trio, check that they have a relationship to a male or female that particularly impressed you.

THE DOE

The factors important in a buck are equally important in a doe. Remember that she passes

many breeding failures in domestic stock. It is usually attributable to less than satisfactory conditions in which the doe is living. The reason may not be one of the actual state of the hutch. Stress, induced by noise, fear or other factors, is a common cause.

Pseudopregnancy: This situation is not uncommon in rabbits. The doe passes through all the stages of apparent pregnancy. She prepares a nest, plucks wool from her chest and her mammary glands swell. However, she is not pregnant. The condition can be induced in a doe living with other females, if she is placed in a hutch previously occupied by a buck or even if she picks up the scent of a buck. Such a doe desires a litter and is in a fertile state. Providing she is in good condition, she should be mated as soon as possible. If she is not mated, be sure she returns to her normal state. If she does not, consult a veterinarian.

MATING

Once your rabbits are in prime condition, mating can commence. Introduce the doe to the buck's hutch--never the reverse. The buck will constantly follow the doe around, indicating his desire to mate. If she is receptive, the doe

Broken Fawn Dwarf Lop rabbit, buck.

Fawn English
Lop rabbit, buck.

will eventually stand so he can mate her. The sexual act is over quickly. However, it may be repeated several times in a short space of time. It is best that you watch the proceedings rather than leave the pair alone together overnight. If the doe is not ready for mating, she will be hounded by the buck for long periods. She may even be attacked. Or, she may turn on the buck and inflict a nasty wound. If it is obvious that mating will not occur that day, return the doe to her hutch. Try again the next day. It is a good idea to pair an inexperienced rabbit with an experienced mate.

Once the mating is over, return the doe to her hutch. Her litter can be expected in about 30 days. Some breeders test mate their does after one week. If she refuses any sort of advances from the buck, the first mating was probably successful.

Litter of rabbits inside their nest. The pregnant doe usually starts building her nest a week before she is due to give birth.

35

Nest box: A doe normally starts to prepare a nest about a week prior to labor. A nest box is not essential, but it does prevent the babies from being scattered around the hutch. A simple box, with the front section low enough to allow easy entrance, is all that is needed. It can be adorned with fresh bedding. The doe will add to this with hair pulled from her chest.

Problems: Things usually go smoothly. Occasionally, though, problems do occur. A maiden doe may be frightened by the birth and ignore the babies. She may scatter them around the nest box and, in the worst of cases, kill the young. Think of anything that may have upset the mother and correct it. If conditions seem ideal, she may just be a bad mother. Do not breed her again.

REARING

Five to six rabbits comprise a normal litter, but up to ten can be produced. Soon after birth, each youngster should be examined with great care. At this time, the doe should be occupied in the hutch or run. Rub your hands over her or in the bedding of her quarters to disguise your scent; if the babies pick up your scent, the mother may kill them. Any deformed youngsters must be culled and the dead removed.

The young are born blind and naked. Their fur begins to grow after four days. Their eyes open around the ninth or tenth day. They emerge from the nest box around three weeks of age and are really cute. At this age, they start to eat various foods. This

process continues until, by about six to eight weeks of age, they are fully weaned and independent of their mother. Remove them from their mother at this time. Be sure to separate the sexes to avoid unwanted matings between siblings.

TAMING

Once the youngsters leave the nest area, they can be handled without too much worry. At this time, they should be picked up and inspected daily. The more they are handled, the tamer they become. Never pick a rabbit up by its ears or tail. Instead, gently encircle the rabbit's abdomen to support its weight with your hand. The bunny can be placed against your chest, with its head looking up to you. Then place your other hand under its rump for further support. The rabbit should feel secure and not struggle.

SEXING

It is difficult to sex very young rabbits with certainty. When they are three months old, the sexual organs will have developed to the point that an

inspection establishes the gender. Place the rabbit on a table or on your lap. Turn the bunny on its back, securing the head with one hand. Gently press on either side of the genitals. A small penis is evident in the male, while a small slit is present in the female. The sexual organs are somewhat further from the anus of the male than of the female. The testes are also apparent in an older male. Be aware that the presence of teats does not indicate gender. Both sexes have teats, though they are more obvious in the female.

Rabbit Breeds

It is estimated that there are over 100 breeds of rabbit. Actually, though, you do not have such a choice because many breeds are available only in their country of origin. Several factors must be considered before a final choice is made. Otherwise, you may end up with a breed unsuited to your needs.

Rare breeds and young rabbits of exhibition standard are more expensive than others. Breeds with long ears or coats require more time than breeds with normal conformations. Very large breeds cost more to keep than do medium and small rabbits. If you plan to breed rabbits, then stick to one breed and one variety, at least initially.

BREED AND VARIETY

A breed of rabbit is defined by its shape, feature or coat. A variety usually refers to the color variations found within a breed. Some breeds are really only varieties of other breeds.

They have developed to such a state that they have their own standards. They are treated as distinct breeds for all practical purposes.

Standard: Each country sets a standard of excellence for the exhibited breeds. This standard is based on the allocation of 100 points. The points are divided between those features considered to be important to that breed. It is wise to obtain a copy of the standard of your country for your chosen breed or variety.

Rabbits come in many colors of the rainbow— there is sure to be something for everyone.

39

FUR OR FANCY

Rabbit breeds are broadly divided into two groups. A rabbit's placement within the group depends on whether it was developed for its fur or as a utility breed. The type and conformation of the rabbit is secondary to the quality of the fur in the fur breeds. Fancy breeds include many older breeds established to provide good pelts and meat. The conformation and fur markings are very important in these fancy breeds. Commercial meat producers had always used the large fancy breeds. Today, meat rabbits are bred from all breeds and crosses of them.

The following descriptions are mostly breeds typically found in pet stores or from breeders. A few rare breeds and meat producers are included. Lesser seen breeds, not mentioned here, are available in Europe and the USA.

Alaska—*Origin:* Germany; Himalayan x Argente x Dutch. *Weight:* 3.6kg (8lbs). *Color:* Black. *Type:* This somewhat rare type has dense, silky fur. The underfur is blue. The nails are black and the eyes black or brown. The body is of short, cobby shape with no apparent neck. The head is foreshortened and round.

American Checkered Giant—*Origin:* Germany; Butterfly breeds x Belgian Hare x Lops. *Weight:* 5.2kg (11.5lbs). *Color:* Black or blue on a white ground color. *Type:* This large breed has a demanding standard. It must have a well arched back, good butterfly smut, even eye circles and a spot on each cheek. There are two spots (or group of spots) on each flank, and a central line down the back.

American—*Origin:*

Netherland Dwarf rabbit, a golden hamster, and a guinea pig.

40

USA; various breeds. *Weight:* 4.5kg (10lbs); there is also a giant variety. *Color:* Blue, White. *Type:* The fur is dense underneath with an overlay of coarse guard hairs. The eyes of a blue are blue; those of a white (albino) are pink.

Angora (English)—*Origin:* probably England. *Weight:* 2.7kg (6lbs); the French breed is grooming to prevent the coat from matting. The wool is highly prized.

Argente De Champagne— *Origin:* France; selective breeding from common stock of the period. *Weight:* 3.6kg (8lbs). *Color:* Silver to pewter gray of even distribution (a darker nose and muzzle are accepted). *Type:* This breed is

Smoke Angora rabbit. This breed is one of the oldest of the fancy rabbits.

heavier. *Color:* White, Agouti, Smoke, Pearl, Chocolate, Cream, Chinchilla, Sable and others. *Type:* A short body with an arched back and a broad chest. The fur in the English is long and silky with fringes (furnishings) on the ears and feet. The French breed has much more dense, but coarser, fur. The Angora needs constant not cobby, but is of moderate length. It has a moderate arch to the back. The ears are medium length. The eyes are brown and the nails are dark to horn color. The fur should be at least 2.54cm (1in) long. Youngsters are a self color when born. The silver coloration takes about six to eight months to show itself. This is probably the oldest

St. Nicholas Blue x Flemish Giant? *Weight:* 3.2kg (7lbs); usually heavier. *Color:* Blue, Black, White, Brown, Lilac. *Type:* The back is longish, showing a dip above the chest. The feet are well developed and the ears are of medium length. The fur is dense and silky. The Whites may have pink, blue or black eyes.

Blanc De Hotot—*Origin:* France; Dutch x Butterfly breeds. *Weight:* 4kg (8.75lbs). *Color:* White with a black eye ring. *Type:* A well balanced and attractive rabbit. The ears are about 12cm (4.75in) long. The black variety is no longer seen.

Black and Tan—*Origin:* England; Dutch x wild rabbits. *Weight:* 2kg (4.5lbs). *Color:* Originally Black on the upper body with contrasting brown on the lower parts, inner ears, eye rings and neck collar. Now available with Blue, Chocolate and Lilac replacing the black. *Type:* This rabbit is similar to the Dutch. It must have a superb coat.

Californian—*Origin:* USA; Himalayan x New Zealand White x Chinchilla. *Weight:* 4.5kg (10lbs). *Color:* White with dark ears, smut, paws and tail. *Type:* The dark extremities

known breed. Two other breeds, the Argente Bleu and Brun, are more cobby in type. The Argente Creme is the smallest of the types. It is a mixture of orange and white.

Belgian Hare—*Origin:* Belgium. The present-day breed is the result of selective breeding in England; it is thought that the original Belgian Hares were descended from the Patagonian or Angevin. *Weight:* 3.8kg (8.5lbs). *Color:* Chestnut. *Type:* A racy, hare-like breed with large ears. The body is lithe and never ungainly. It requires a lot of exercise. The fur is ticked with black. The eyes are hazel. This is a giant breed reputed to have reached lengths of 1.5m (5ft).

Beveren—*Origin:* Belgium;

may be black or chocolate. This large rabbit was developed for its meat and pelt potential.

Chinchilla—*Origin:* France; Himalayan x Beveren x wild rabbit. Since its development, other breeds have been used in attempts to improve it. These include the Black and Tan, Angora, Siamese and Marten Sables. *Weight:* 2.7kg (6lbs). *Color:* Chinchilla, resembling that of the chinchilla of South America. The underfur is dark slate blue. The midlayer is pearl edged by black. The top coat is light gray ticked with white.

There are now Blue, Iron Gray and Brown varieties. *Type:* The fur must be dense, soft and fine. This is a short, cobby breed with fine bone structure. The ears are tight together at the base. The Chinchilla has been used to improve fur in numerous breeds.

Cinnamon—*Origin:* USA; the exact breeds used are not known. *Weight:* 4.3kg (9.5lbs). *Color:* Cinnamon or Rust with smoke gray ticking on the back. Two rust markings should be inside the rear legs. The extremities should be of darker

Broken Chinchilla Dwarf Lop rabbit.

color than the body. *Type:* This is a well muscled, plump looking breed. Any white hair in the coat is a bad fault, as are blotchy markings. The eyes are hazel.

Dutch—*Origin:* Belgium; Brabancon x English Piebald breeds. *Weight:* 2.3kg (5lbs).

Color: Black, Blue, Steel Gray, Pale Gray, Brown Gray, Tortoise, Chocolate and Yellow. In each case, the color is contrasted against white. The line of demarcation between the color and the white must be as straight as possible. The cheek patches must not intrude beyond the cheeks. The white blaze should go to a "V" at the base of the ears. The white rear foot stops should extend about 3cm (1.25in) up the feet and end in a straight line. *Type:* This is a neat, cobby little rabbit. Its rounded, compact shape, oval head, medium length, erect ears and characteristic coat pattern make it identifiable the world over. The Dutch is an ideal pet rabbit. It combines good looks with a gentle nature and small size.

English Spot (USA) or English Butterfly (UK)—*Origin:* England; selective breeding from stock of the period. *Weight:* 3kg (7lbs). *Color:* The ground color is white. The markings may be Black, Blue, Tortoise and Gray. The colors should form a butterfly smut on the nose, an unbroken chain of herringbone markings along the spine and a chain of progressively larger

spots commencing behind the ears and running down each flank to the tail. *Type:* These are longer looking rabbits than the Dutch. When lying down, they exhibit a gentle arch to the back.

English Silver—*Origin:* Some researchers says France, others say England. *Weight:* 2.7kg (6lbs). *Color:* Silver Gray, Silver Fawn, Silver Brown. *Type:* A medium sized rabbit with fine bone structure.

Flemish Giant—*Origin:* Belgium. *Weight:* 5.4kg (12lbs). *Color:* Black, Blue, Fawn, Light Gray, Sandy, Steel Gray, White. *Type:* This is a large, cylindrical breed. It has long ears. The fur is dense and sleek. It is the largest of all domestic breeds.

Florida White—*Origin:* USA; Polish x Dutch x New Zealand White. *Weight:* 2.5kg (5lbs). *Color:* Pure White. *Type:* This breed is a true albino with pink eyes. It is a compact, cobby rabbit. The ears are medium to short.

Harlequin—*Origin:* France; from tricolor Dutch rabbits of the Brabancon type. *Weight:* 3.2kg (7lbs). *Color:* Black and Orange, Blue and Fawn, Brown and Orange, Gray and Fawn, Black and White, Blue and White, Brown and White, Gray and White. Those with white on the body are known as magpies. The arrangement of the colors is complex. One ear must be of a different color than the other. The face on the same side should contrast the ear. The shoulder and feet should be opposite to this. The rear foot on the same side is the opposite color of the front foot. A band of color should encircle the body. *Type:* A medium sized rabbit with large ears. The coat is dense and sleek. The fur may be normal, rex or astrex.

Havana—*Origin:* Holland; Himalayan x local common

An Arctic Hare in its summer coat.

45

stock. *Weight:* 2.7kg (6lbs). *Color:* Dark Chocolate with a sheen of purple. The underbelly is gray. *Type:* Originally there were larger, longer types. A smaller, more cobby variety is preferred today. The Havana is often used to improve the fur of other breeds.

Himalayan—*Origin:* Unknown. *Weight:* 2.3kg (5lbs). *Color:* The ground color is white. The extremities may be Black, Chocolate, Blue or Lilac. *Type:* This is a small to medium sized breed. The body is described as snaky yet elegant.

The ears should be narrow and short. The eyes are pink.

Lilac—*Origin:* Belgium; Havana x Beveren x ? *Weight:* 2.9kg (6.5lbs). *Color:* A Pinky Dove which must be carried right down to the skin. *Type:* Similar to the Havana, this is a nicely compacted breed. Color and a dense, silky coat are the key factors of a good Lilac.

Lop—*Origin:* England. *Weight:* 3.4kg (7.5lbs). *Color:* Any color. *Type:* The main feature of a lop is its enormous ears. The width and shape of the ear are also important.

Netherland Dwarf—*Origin:* England or Holland. *Weight:* .9kg (2lbs). *Color:* This breed is available in just about every color and coat pattern. The standard divides this breed into five groups: 1) Selfs: White, Black, Brown, Lilac; 2) Shadeds: Sable Siamese, Smoke Pearl Siamese; 3) Agoutis: Chestnut with black ticking, Opal, Lynx, Chinchilla, Squirrel; 4) Tan Patterned: Black, Blue, Chocolate, Lilac; 5) other varieties: Orange, Fawn, Tortoise, Steel Blue, Himalayan. *Type:* The dwarf is a cobby little rabbit with a round head. The eyes are large and round. The tiny ears are

A young Frosty-point Holland Lop female rabbit.

erect and slightly rounded.

New Zealand—*Origin:* USA. *Weight:* 5.4kg (12lbs). *Color:* Red, White, Black. *Type:* These large rabbits are

White, Black, Chocolate. *Type:* It has a compact body and large, round eyes. The short ears are erect. The coat is short, fine and lays close to the body.

bred mainly for their meat.

Palomino—*Origin:* USA. *Weight:* 4.3kg (9.5lbs). *Color:* Golden, Lynx. *Type:* A well balanced breed of medium size. The ears are medium size to complement the body size.

Polish—*Origin:* England. *Weight:* 1.1kg (2.5lbs). *Color:*

Rex—*Origin:* France. *Weight:* 3.2kg (7lbs). *Color:* Black, Blue, Californian, Castor, Chinchilla, Chocolate, Lilac, Lynx, Opal, Red, Sable, Seal, White. *Type:* The outstanding feature of the Rex is its fur. The guard hairs are the same length as the undercoat.

Fawn Rex rabbit.

47

Marten Sable Dwarf rabbit.

The effect makes the fur look and feel like velvet. The body and ears are of medium size.

Rhinelander—*Origin:* Germany; English Butterfly (spot) x Harlequin. *Weight:* 3.8kg (8.5lbs). *Color:* Tricolor, white background with black and orange spots. *Type:* This is a thick-set breed exhibiting well-rounded proportions.

Sable—*Origin:* France; Chinchilla x Angora. *Weight:* 2.7kg (6lbs). *Color:* The two varieties, the Marten and the Siamese, are divided into light, medium and dark Sables. *Type:* The Sable is a smart, medium sized rabbit. The ears are small to medium.

Satin—*Origin:* USA; a mutation of the Havana. *Weight:* 3.2kg (7lbs). *Color:* Virtually all colors and coat patterns. *Type:* A compact, cobby rabbit. The Satin gene is an autosomal recessive in mode of transmission. The coat is extremely smooth with superb luster.

Siberian—*Origin:* England. *Weight:* 2.7kg (6lbs). *Color:*

Black, Blue, Brown, Lilac. *Type:* A medium sized breed with a short neck. The fur is dense and has a high sheen. The ears are medium in length.

Silver Fox—*Origin:* England and Germany; Black and Tan x Chinchilla. *Weight:* 2.7kg (6lbs). *Color:* Black, Blue, Chocolate, Lilac. The base color is contrasted with white or a pale version of the base color. The pattern resembles the Black and Tan breed.

Silver Fox (American)—*Origin:* USA; Silver x Self Checkered Giants. *Weight:* 5.4kg (12lbs). *Color:* Black or Blue tipped with white hairs. *Type:* This is a large breed. The extremities are usually slightly darker than the body.

Smoke Pearl—*Origin:* Scotland. *Weight:* 2.7kg (6lbs). *Color:* Smoke shading to pearl gray on the lower parts distinguish this breed. There are Marten and Siamese varieties of coat pattern. *Type:* Similar to the Sable.

A Smoke Pearl Brittania Petite rabbit. This breed is the British version of the Polish rabbit.

49

Health

It is better to avoid illness rather than having to treat it. Probably over half of all rabbit ailments are partly or wholly attributable to poor husbandry. Just consider the multitude of potential causes of spreading disease, creating stress and reducing a rabbit's natural resistance to illness: drafty accommodations, inadequate diets, unclean feeding dishes, contaminated foods, overcrowding, lack of exercise, poor breeding. Each one of these aspects can induce an illness and then cause it to spread.

Even in the best run of rabbits, though, there is always a risk of infection. Many diseases are airborne, are transmitted via bird droppings or are introduced by an owner who has come in contact with an ill animal. Every precaution must be taken to simply keep the risks down to an acceptable level. If a feeding pot or water bottle has a crack, replace it. If a hutch wire is rusty, renew it.

(heating pad, light bulb) to keep the animal warm. The cage should be large enough to allow the rabbit to move into or away from the heat source as required. Heat is an excellent remedy in itself. It also induces thirst. Since numerous drugs can be supplied via the drinking water, this is a good way to administer medication. After each use, the contaminated hospital cage must be carefully disinfected. Therefore, be sure to keep the ailing bunny warm and consult the following list of likely problems and remedies.

Antibiotics: Use of antibiotics on rabbits must be done under veterinary supervision. The fact that a rabbit requires certain bacteria in its stomach for digestion means that antibiotics can be counter-productive. The medications might destroy essential bacteria and allow others, which are not beneficial, to flourish.

Bloat: This is typically the result of excess green food. A build-up of gases in the stomach occurs from fermentation being

Black Silver Fox rabbit. Getting acquainted with your pet will help you realize when something is wrong with him.

Do not keep lawn trimmings rotting in a pile near a hutch. It is a breeding place for parasites and germs. Clean the hutches at least once a week. Remove uneaten food daily. Do not introduce newly acquired stock into your run until they have undergone three weeks of quarantine.

Should a rabbit become ill, isolate it from the rest of the stock immediately. The isolation or hospital cage should be fitted with a heat source unable to escape. A mild laxative should help because the rabbit is also constipated. The condition is less likely to occur if more, but smaller, meals are fed.

Canker: Constant scratching of the ear indicates a problem. An inspection may reveal hard, brown wax. This is caused by mites whose life cycle is completed on the host. Treatment with benzyl benzoate or a similar acaricide is effective. The nymphs must be killed as they hatch, before reaching the reproductive age. Single treatments are incompetent. Treat for three to four weeks.

Coccidiosis: This is an acute form of diarrhea. It may also affect the liver. Essentially, however, it is an intestinal problem created by microscopic protozoans of the genera *Eimeria* and *Isospora*. They attack the lining of the gut. The disease is highly contagious, so infected stock quickly pass on the problem to others. Young rabbits who have not yet built up a natural immunity are most at risk. The condition is often the result of overcrowding and poor hygiene. Rabbits in such

Broken Fawn Holland Lop rabbit. Note the clean fur on this bunny.

an environment eat fouled food containing parasites. Treatment is rendered by using sulfur based drugs.

Diarrhea: Reduce green foods immediately and maintain meticulous hygiene. Persistent diarrhea should be reported to your veterinarian. Diarrhea is often a symptom of another manifestation. Microscopic examination of the feces confirms the cause.

Fleas and Lice: Check the fur for these parasites. Fleas are seen as tiny, reddish, mobile creatures. The rabbit flea,

Spilopsyllus cuniculi, is believed to be the main carrier of myxomatosis. So if you live in an area where this dreaded disease is still present, constant vigilance is needed. Lice are seen as tiny gray specks. Their eggs are whitish in color. They do not move around a great deal. Usually the back, head and ears of the rabbit are infested. Fleas and lice are both easily eradicated by using acaracides. Infestations can be totally avoided by clean living conditions and regular inspection of the stock.

A pair of Dutch rabbits. If one of your rabbits is ill, isolate it immediately.

Fungal Infections (Ringworm): This is a stubborn problem to combat. The signs are skin lesions encrusted with a flaky layer. The cause is the fungus *Trichophyton*. A wholly satisfactory treatment is not available. Iodine, ammonium compounds, oils and soaps have all been used with moderate success. All bedding material must be burned and the hutches must be cleaned with disinfectant. Unfortunately, this fungus can survive for months without a host.

Heat Stroke: During very hot weather, rabbits may be seen panting, staggering about and even vomiting. Large rabbits and those with foreshortened faces are the most likely to be affected. Place a cold, wet towel around the rabbit and move it to a cool place. The best prevention is a shaded, well ventilated area. Provide cool drinking water and periodically dampen the hutch with water. A jug of ice in the hutch also helps to keep the animals cool.

Hay Poisoning: Milkweed, a plant found in meadows of the USA, causes this condition. The rabbit is paralyzed, especially its head and back (which becomes arched). The extent of the condition depends upon how much milkweed was ingested. Consult your veterinarian.

Maggots: During warm weather, flies and other winged insects may lay eggs in the rabbits' fecal matter. Rabbits in poor condition have feces clinging to their fur. The eggs hatch and the larvae burrow into a rabbit's tissue. Toxic chemicals are released. Secondary infections are induced as the rabbit scratches and creates wounds. Check your rabbits daily to remove any fecal matter. Wipe an infected area with a mild disinfectant or acaricide.

Mites: Mites can be spread to and from various animals. So be wary if you own other pets. Mites are tiny arthropods which move on the skin's surface or burrow into it. Mites often hide in crevices of the hutch during the day, and emerge to feed on the rabbit's blood at night. Lesions appear on the skin. Some mites are harmless to the host but carry other debilitating bacteria. Mites are easily eradicated with an acaricide. Heavy infestation is the result of poor husbandry.

Overgrown Nails and Teeth: Invest in a pair of guillotine clippers if a rabbit's claws appear too long. Trim back the nail, being careful not to cut the quick. The quick is the blood vessel supplying nutrients to the nail. If the quick is cut, it is painful and bleeds

profusely. Look underneath the nails to get a good idea where the vein ends. It may be helpful if two people attend to this procedure. One holds the rabbit while the other cuts. If you are unsure about your proficiency, consult a veterinarian. Supply plenty of hard materials (tree branches, wooden blocks) to prevent overgrown teeth. A veterinarian may need to trim the teeth occasionally. Do not breed rabbits exhibiting this fault.

Marten Sable rabbit showing a heavy molt.

Pasteurellosis: This term covers a range of diseases found in birds and mammals. A mild form is commonly seen in rabbits. Known as snuffles, it is restricted to the respiratory tract. It is caused by the bacteria *Pasteurella multocida*, or a related species. A rabbit is constantly pawing at its nose. The inner side of the front legs are wet and stained from nasal discharge. Treatment is difficult, but sulfonamides are the probably the most effective. More acute forms spread to the digestive and reproductive systems. Death normally follows. Surviving animals may become carriers, so they are best destroyed.

Pseudotuberculosis: This disease occurs in many animals, especially rabbits, rodents and birds. Treat it with importance because it is transmissible to humans. Unfortunately, it is not always clinically apparent until the late stages. The symptoms may be no more than loose feces and reduced appetite. More advanced stages may exhibit nasal discharge, labored breathing, bloodstained droppings and weight loss. It affects most internal organs. Broad spectrum antibiotics may reduce the effects of the disease, but there is no cure.

Pneumonia: The symptoms of pneumonia are much like the early symptoms of pseudotuberculosis. If caught early, pneumonia can be cleared up with veterinary treatment. However, the vet cannot cure the cause: drafty housing, a faulty diet and poor husbandry.

Salmonellosis: This intestinal disease is not common in rabbits. However, a rabbit can die from it without ever having displayed any particularly worrying symptoms. Sometimes the disease can only be diagnosed by microscopy. If a rabbit dies without an apparent illness, have post mortem done by a vet. Birds and rodents are well-known carriers of the disease.

Slobbers: This aptly named condition results from bad teeth or a mouth ulcer or abscess. Each causes a rabbit to discharge excessive amounts of saliva. Unless it is symptomatic of another, more serious disease, veterinary treatment should cure the problem.

Vent Disease: Small blisters develop around the vent. They become more widespread and develop scabs. Consult a veterinarian for the proper treatment. After a two to three week period, the rabbit can be returned to the hutch.

Worms: Various internal worms afflict mammals and birds. They are no problem under normal conditions. Problems begin when infestations of them build up. They reduce the benefits a rabbit receives from its food. General debility then induces other problems. If evidence of worms is seen in the droppings or is vomited up, consult your vet.

Wounds: Minor cuts can be wiped with a mild disinfectant. They usually heal rapidly. More serious wounds should be dressed and treated by a veterinarian. The most difficult problem is keeping the dressing on the rabbit.

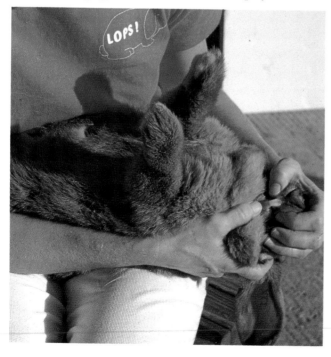

Lop rabbit having its incisors checked. If your pet's teeth are overgrown, take it to your veterinarian.

Showing Rabbits

GROOMING

The grooming of most rabbit breeds is a simple matter, because the majority of rabbits have short fur. This does not imply that grooming can be ignored for long periods. A rabbit must be groomed at least once a week. In this way, the fur is kept in peak condition. Also, you will be aware if parasites infect your pet.

Brushing and Combing: A stiff bristle brush and a fine-toothed metal comb are needed. Bristle is preferred to nylon, as the latter tends to create static electricity. Give the rabbit's coat a brisk brushing in the direction of the hair to remove tangles. Be sure to include the chest and underbelly. Next, comb the fur in the same direction. A final polish with a chamois leather adds luster.

Bathing: Use a mild pet soap to prevent excessive drying of

the skin and fur. Be sure to rinse the rabbit thoroughly to remove all traces of soap. After bathing, give a good toweling. A blow dryer set on a low temperature can be used to hasten drying. A damp rabbit should certainly be

A well-groomed rabbit like this one makes a much more cheerful pet than a bunny that is unkempt.

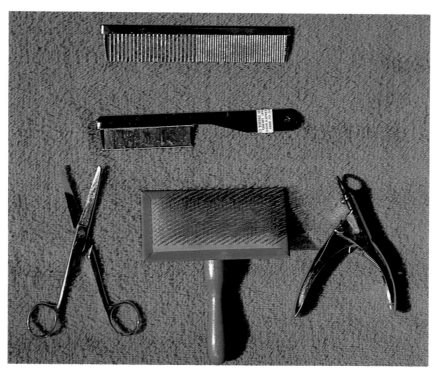

kept in a warm, draft-proof environment.

Molting: Rabbits molt or shed their hair once a year. The molt normally commences in the spring and is completed by the summer. Regular grooming removes dead hairs to allow the new coat to come through quicker and better.

Grooming Angoras: An Angora rabbit needs special attention to keep the coat from becoming matted. It requires grooming every day to look its best. If you shampoo the rabbit, ensure that all tangles are removed before bathing. Special anti-tangle lotions available for dogs are also suitable for Angoras.

Grooming Lops: The ears of Lop rabbits need regular washing or wiping. They may

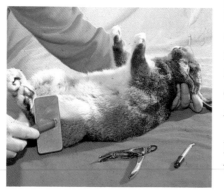

be towel dried and then powdered. This is then brushed out of the fur with a soft bristle brush. The nails of the Lop must be kept short to prevent scratching of the ears.

EXHIBITIONS

The rabbit show is the logical conclusion to a breeding program. Here you find out just how your stock compares with that of other enthusiasts. Additionally, you will learn much about rabbits and meet people with a common interest.

Rabbit Organizations: The rabbit shows of each country are governed by a national ruling body. This unit lays down the standards of excellence for each breed. They administrate all matters from supreme awards, to registration of stock, to complaints. I strongly recommend that you join a club affiliated with these units. It is worth your while to get a copy of the standards set forth for your breed and a copy of the show rules. Also, you

Perfect example of a rabbit going through the molt. A good brushing is imperative at this time.

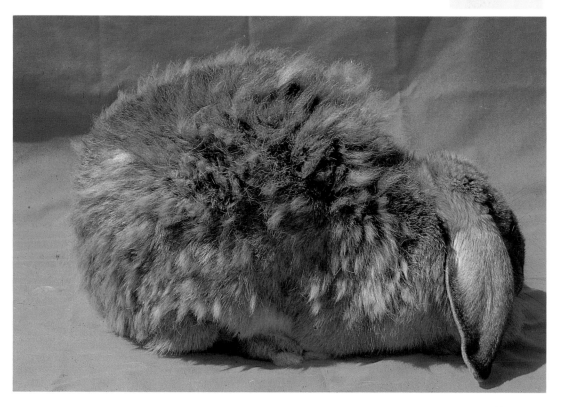

might be interested in receiving magazines or other publications about rabbits. The addresses of your nearest clubs or societies are obtainable from the secretary of the national club.

Types of Clubs: You may join a rabbit club which caters to all breeds. Alternatively, you may prefer a specialty club which caters to just your breed. Membership fees are quite modest. Many breeders are members of two or more clubs.

Index